BOOKS IN THIS SERIES

1. **THE DIARY OF AMOS LEE**
   I Sit, I Write, I Flush!

2. **THE DIARY OF AMOS LEE**
   Girls, Guts and Glory!

3. **THE DIARY OF AMOS LEE**
   I'm Twelve, I'm Tough, I Tweet!

ALSO BY ADELINE FOO

1. **WHOOPIE LEE**
   Almost Famous

THE DIARY OF AMOS LEE

Your D.I.Y. Toilet Diary to Fame!

Written by
ADELINE FOO

Illustrated by
STEPHANIE WONG

E

EPIGRAM BOOKS / SINGAPORE

FIRST PRINTING, 2012
Text © Adeline Foo 2011
Illustrations © Epigram 2011

PUBLISHED BY EPIGRAM BOOKS
1008 Toa Payoh North #03-08 Singapore 318996
Tel: (65) 6292 4456 / Fax: (65) 6292 4414
enquiry@epigrambooks.sg / www.epigrambooks.sg

ILLUSTRATIONS AND COVER DESIGN BY
Stephanie Wong

NATIONAL LIBRARY BOARD SINGAPORE
CATALOGUING IN PUBLICATION DATA
Foo, Adeline, 1971-
The Diary of Amos Lee: Your D.I.Y. Toilet Dairy to Fame!/written by Adeline Foo,
illustrated by Stephanie Wong. – Singapore: Epigram Books, 2011.
p. cm.
ISBN-13: 978-981-07-0757-6 (pbk.)

1. Boys – Singapore – Diaries – Juvenile fiction.
2. Do-it-yourself work – Juvenile fiction. I. Wong, Stephanie, 1979- II. Title.

PZ7
S823 – dc22 OCN760937377

Printed in Singapore.

iNSTRUCTiONS:

- Write in the toilet before you wipe your bottom (duh, must I explain why?).

- You're only allowed five minutes per page (or when you're done with bombing, whichever comes first).

- If you see a question or activity that stumps you, skip to the next page!

- Answer all questions in the personality tests as truthfully as you can.

- Keep this diary safe, don't let it fall in the hands of a sibling.

- Keep it clean and dry in a secret place (like in your underwear drawer, or where your mother keeps the dictionary).

- If you develop piles from spending too much time in the toilet with this book, don't blame me!

People call me Famous Amos. How original! It was Mum's idea to name me after her favourite cookies, and now, I'm stuck with it. But fame isn't a bad thing, it gets you attention. I've read that famous celebrities start their road to fame as young as 12! Christina Aguilera and Justin Timberlake were 12 when they competed in auditions to get into The New Mickey Mouse Club. Justin Bieber was only 12 when his first performance posted on YouTube got ten million views. Imagine that! Twelve and already famous! Today, they are famous stars who are pop culture idols for their many fans. So how did they groom themselves to fame? They must have started somewhere.

I like to think that as Singapore's Most Famous Toilet Diarist, I am qualified to share how you can get started on the road to fame. This D.I.Y. diary is peppered with activities, doodles and personality tests to check if you're ready for it. Answer all the questions as truthfully as you can. You will be amazed at what you will learn about yourself.

And in case you're wondering why Whoopie, a.k.a. WPI, the whiny, pesky and irritating sister of mine, is also credited on the cover of this book, it's because I'm feeling generous. No kidding.

Aaalright... that's not quite true. Mum said that she has found a publisher who's willing to publish this D.I.Y. Diary. The only problem is, I'm short on ideas. Then Whoopie suggested she can add some lines! I thought, why not? More lines mean more ideas, and with more pages, I'll get paid more! Yeah!

So here's the deal, use this diary, fill it with honest answers and draw as much as you want! But keep it safe. One day when you've made it, who knows, you might be the next Prime Minister of Singapore, or maybe a famous movie star or singer, remember that it was Amos Lee who taught you how to get on the road to fame. Start writing now. Have fun and good luck!

ADOPT A COOL NAME!

Do You Have a Unique Name?

Here's a test. Do you know five other people with the same name? Well, if you do, tough luck! You're not going to stand out when the Movie Director calls out your name in an audition. So what should you do? Here's a quick fix.

Write your name:

Mhain   Annie

E.g. A n g e l i n e.
Replace the last letter with a different vowel
(either a, e, i, o, or u), Angelina, Angelini, Angelino, Angelinu...

Mhairio   Anniza

Read the name out aloud. Do you like how it "sounds"
and "looks"?

You can adopt this as a stage name, or here's another
idea, you can give your pet hamster this new name!
So the next time you turn up for an audition with 200
other Angelines, tell the Casting Director that you're the
only Angeline with a pet hamster named Angelini. Bet you
will really stand out!

Here's Another Tip
Write your name:

Mhairi   Annie

E.g. S e b a s t i a n
Add a "z" to your name, it adds pizzazz!
S e b a s t i a n z

Mhairiz   Anniez

Sign Your Name As an Autograph

Trace the letters (of the alphabet) given here. Isn't it fun? You can almost pretend you're back in kindergarten, learning to write in cursive for the first time, aaha!

Aa Bb Cc Dd

Ee Ff Gg Hh

Ii Jj Kk Ll

Mm Nn Oo Pp

Qq Rr Ss Tt

Uu Vv Ww Xx

Yy Zz

Practise signing your autograph here!

7

Here is the first thing you must do!
Get your family members to sign their names!
Don't forget your friends too!

2

KNOW YOUR
STAR SIGN

Did You Know?

The Zodiac is the imaginary band in the heavens marked out by a path of the sun with eight degrees to either side. It is broken into 12 segments, each symbolised by a star sign (Zodia, which means "little beasts"). These star signs take on fixed periods within the year and each star sign is associated with certain characteristics:

Aries (Ram) Mar 21 - Apr 20
You are a born leader and a good speaker!

Characteristics:
Confident and courageous.

Taurus (Bull) Apr 21 - May 20
You love nature and the outdoors!

Characteristics:
Outgoing and friendly.

Gemini (Twins) May 21 - Jun 20
You are witty and popular among friends!

Characteristics:
Chatty and full of vigour.

Cancer (Crab) Jun 21 - Jul 22
You tend to be protective of those you love.

Characteristics:
Creative and artistic.

Leo (Lion) Jul 23 - Aug 22
You are loyal to friends and loved ones,
you're fun to hang out with!

Characteristics:
Enjoys being the centre of attention.

Virgo (Virgin) Aug 23 - Sep 22
You have a great sense of humour.
Some Virgos are also athletic and talented
in sports.

Characteristics:
Motivated and enjoys excelling.

Libra (Scales) Sep 23 - Oct 22
You are an artistic intellectual and have
a playful nature.

Characteristics:
Energetic and playful.

Scorpio (Scorpion) Oct 23 - Nov 22
You are strong-willed and determined to excel!

Characteristics:
Independent and competitive.

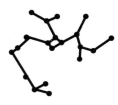

Sagittarius (Archer) Nov 23 - Dec 21
You are sociable and full of energy,
everyone likes you!

Characteristics:
Friendly and adapts easily to change.

Capricorn (Sea-goat) Dec 22 - Jan 19
You are analytical and like doing things
systematically.

Characteristics:
Logical in thinking and likes to plan ahead.

Aquarius (Water Bearer) Jan 20 - Feb 19
You are dependable and smart.

Characteristics:
Responsible and organised.

Pisces (Fish) Feb 20 - Mar 20
You are sensitive and feel strongly
for people you care about.

Characteristics:
Intuitive and sensitive to moods.

The general traits of people born under the star signs
vary. But if you look at your favourite pop stars, celebrities
or storybook characters and check out their star signs,
that will give you something to smile about.

If you're lucky enough to be born under the same
constellation, it gives you a thrill, doesn't it?

Make a Birthday List of your friends and family.
Who shares your star sign?

♈ aries
Mar 21 - Apr 20

Name	Birthday
Lady Gaga (Famous singer)	28 Mar 1986
Jackie Chan (Movie star)	7 Apr 1954
Leonardo Da Vinci (The artist, not the Ninja Turtle)	15 Apr 1452
Emma Watson (Hermione, *Harry Potter*)	15 Apr 1990

♉ TAURUS

Apr 21 - May 20

Name	Birthday
Queen Elizabeth II	21 Apr 1926
Kelly Clarkson (First *American Idol* winner)	24 Apr 1982
David Beckham (Football star)	2 May 1975
George Lucas (Director of *Star Wars*)	14 May 1944

Name	Birthday
Kylie Minogue (Singer)	28 May 1968
Angelina Jolie (Movie star)	4 Jun 1975
Paula Abdul (Former *American Idol* judge)	19 Jun 1962

II gemini

May 21 - Jun 20

Name	Birthday
Rebecca Black (Famous YouTube sensation)	21 Jun 1997
Prince William	21 Jun 1982
Tom Hanks (The voice of Woody in *Toy Story*)	9 Jul 1956

Cancer

Jun 21 - Jul 22

♌ Leo

Jul 23 - Aug 22

Name	Birthday
Selena Gomez (Justin Bieber's current girlfriend)	22 Jul 1992
Daniel Radcliffe (Harry Potter)	23 Jul 1989
J.K. Rowling (You MUST know her!)	31 Jul 1965
Barack Obama (Who? Just kidding. The President of USA. DUH!)	4 Aug 1961

Name	Birthday
Michael Jackson (King of Pop)	29 Aug 1958
Lea Michele (Rachel Berry, *Glee*)	29 Aug 1986
Beyoncé Knowles (Famous singer)	4 Sep 1981
Roald Dahl (You don't read enough if you don't know him!)	13 Sep 1916

♍

Virgo

Aug 23 - Sep 22

Name	Birthday
Hilary Duff (Famous singer and actress)	28 Sep 1987
Amos Lee (That's me)	1 Oct 1999
Simon Cowell (Who?)	7 Oct 1959
Zac Efron (Famous actor)	18 Oct 1987

♏ SCORPIO

Oct 23 - Nov 22

Name	Birthday
Gordon Ramsay (Why would I care?)	8 Nov 1966
Neil Gaiman (Er, who?)	10 Nov 1960
Katy Perry (Awesome singer!)	25 Oct 1984
Bill Gates (He created Microsoft)	28 Oct 1955

Name	Birthday
Miley Cyrus (*Hannah Montana*)	23 Nov 1992
Whoopie Lee (WPI, Only "Almost Famous")	12 Dec 2002
Taylor Swift (*Famous singer*)	13 Dec 1989

♐

Sagittarius
Nov 23 - Dec 21

♑
CAPRICORN
Dec 22 - Jan 19

Name	Birthday
Elvis Presley (King of Rock and Roll)	8 Jan 1935
Michelle Obama (The woman behind the US President)	17 Jan 1964
Logan Wade Lerman (*Percy Jackson*)	19 Jan 1992

aquarius

Jan 20 - Feb 19

Name	Birthday
Justin Timberlake (Before Justin Bieber, he was cool)	31 Jan 1981
Taylor Lautner (Jacob Black, *Twilight*)	11 Feb 1992
Zachary Gordon (*Diary of a Wimpy Kid*)	15 Feb 1998
Paris Hilton (Who?)	17 Feb 1981

Name	Birthday
Drew Barrymore (Famous actress)	22 Feb 1975
Steve Jobs (Founder of Apple and the iphone)	24 Feb 1955
Justin Bieber (He rocks!)	1 Mar 1994

⧛ pisces

Feb 20 - Mar 20

read your fingers!

Fingers, we need them to hold and grip, they are "tools" that help us retrieve things or communicate with others. But do you know that in palmistry (the study of lines on the palm to read one's fortune), fingers are given names derived from the gods of Roman mythology? Awesome, right?

Drum roll please... ta-da,
meet Jupiter, Saturn, Apollo and Mercury!

Did you know that the length of your fingers indicate
traits of your personality? The longer your finger is, the
stronger the trait!

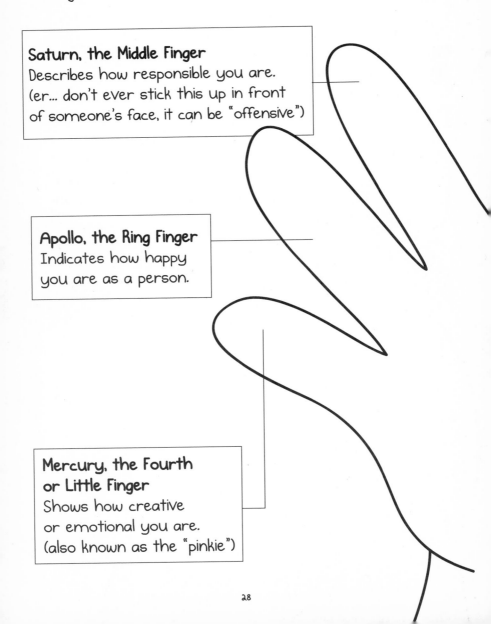

Saturn, the Middle Finger
Describes how responsible you are.
(er... don't ever stick this up in front
of someone's face, it can be "offensive")

Apollo, the Ring Finger
Indicates how happy
you are as a person.

**Mercury, the Fourth
or Little Finger**
Shows how creative
or emotional you are.
(also known as the "pinkie")

Jupiter, the Index Finger
Describes leadership abilities and assertiveness.

Thumb, the Neglected Cousin
Now in case you're wondering why the poor thumb hasn't got a name, don't ask me. But I can guess why. If you were a Roman god, would you want to lend your name to the shortest digit on the hand?

But don't thumb your nose on the thumb (er... no pun intended). It's one of the most important units of the hand. As an "opposable" thumb, it allows us to grip on to something. Do a clawing action with your fingers, do you see that your thumb is below the fingers?

This allows you to "grab and grip", a trait which only primates like monkeys and men share.

Trace Your Right Palm
(If you can't hold the pencil with your left hand,
get someone to do it for you, duh!)

Is Your Apollo Finger Long?

If it is, congratulations!
This finger reads your potential
for fame. If it's long, you're
likely to be a celebrity, oh yeah!
But be warned, if it's really,
really long, what it means is
that you crave to be notorious,
or infamous, as my Mum would
say (i.e. evil or wicked).

YOUR FAMILY MEMBERS – ARE THEY ONE OF THE BIG FIVE?

List all the members in your family.
Think of an animal that best describes
their behaviour.

For example: (left to right)
Your sister, the Pesky Mosquito.
Grandma, the Busy Ant.
Grandpa, the Wise Owl.
Dad, the Sweet-natured Bear.
Mum, the Fearsome Tigress.

List and draw all the members in your family as the
animal that best describes their behaviour.

MUM Queenbee
Dad sire Cheeta
Me - anyhting

Do you have any of them falling in the category of the Big Five? These are the lion, elephant, cape buffalo, leopard, and rhinoceros associated with African wildlife.

Well, if you ever become famous, you can rest assured that the Big Five will come in handy to fend for you as your talent manager. You can only trust your family when it comes to managing your career. Mum's the best, if I may say. She got me this writing job to have my diary published, didn't she?

5 GOT A PET?

Forget the usual suspects like dogs, cats, rabbits, guinea pigs or terrapins. If you can stomach rearing a tarantula, rat, or cockroach, congratulations, you're on the road to fame! Better still, if your pet falls under the "Reptile Group", like a snake, gecko or iguana! The more exotic it is, the higher is your star factor. Imagine this, when you show up for an audition with your pet, everyone's going to keep you at arm's length. Then you'd have drawn attention to yourself! Brilliant, right?

List your top three favourite pets

Dog, cat hamster

guinhea Pig

Paste a picture of your pet or a friend's pet that you think is cool!

If you don't have a pet, create one... the stranger the better. Try drawing your make-believe pet.

If your mother refuses to let a pet into the flat, well, the next best thing you can do is to draw and colour it well. Have a picture of your pet framed and hung up on the wall. When you're famous and can call the shots, you can bring it home!

6
We are
THE 3As!

Form a Buddy Group!

Do you have friends with amazing talents? Maybe someone who's a whiz at computers, like Anthony, or Alvin, who swims like a crocodile is after him in the pool.

My Mum always tells me to stick with people who have a positive zeal for life. These are friends who will stand by you when you're in trouble or comfort you when you're down. It's fun to form a buddy group! You cultivate a sense of belonging and you can do stuff that all of you enjoy, like watch a movie, share books and play computer games together.

List names of friends you would invite for your buddy group!

_____   _____

_____   _____

_____   _____

Write down a name for your buddy group.

_____

_____

Write down a secret slogan that all members of the
buddy group must remember.

_____

_____

Arrange to meet once a week. Remember the secret
slogan to get into the buddy group meeting, and no siblings
are allowed! Suggest a few places for your meetings.

_____   _____

_____   _____

_____   _____

_____   _____

Draw or paste a buddy group photo!

7

create a
fact page

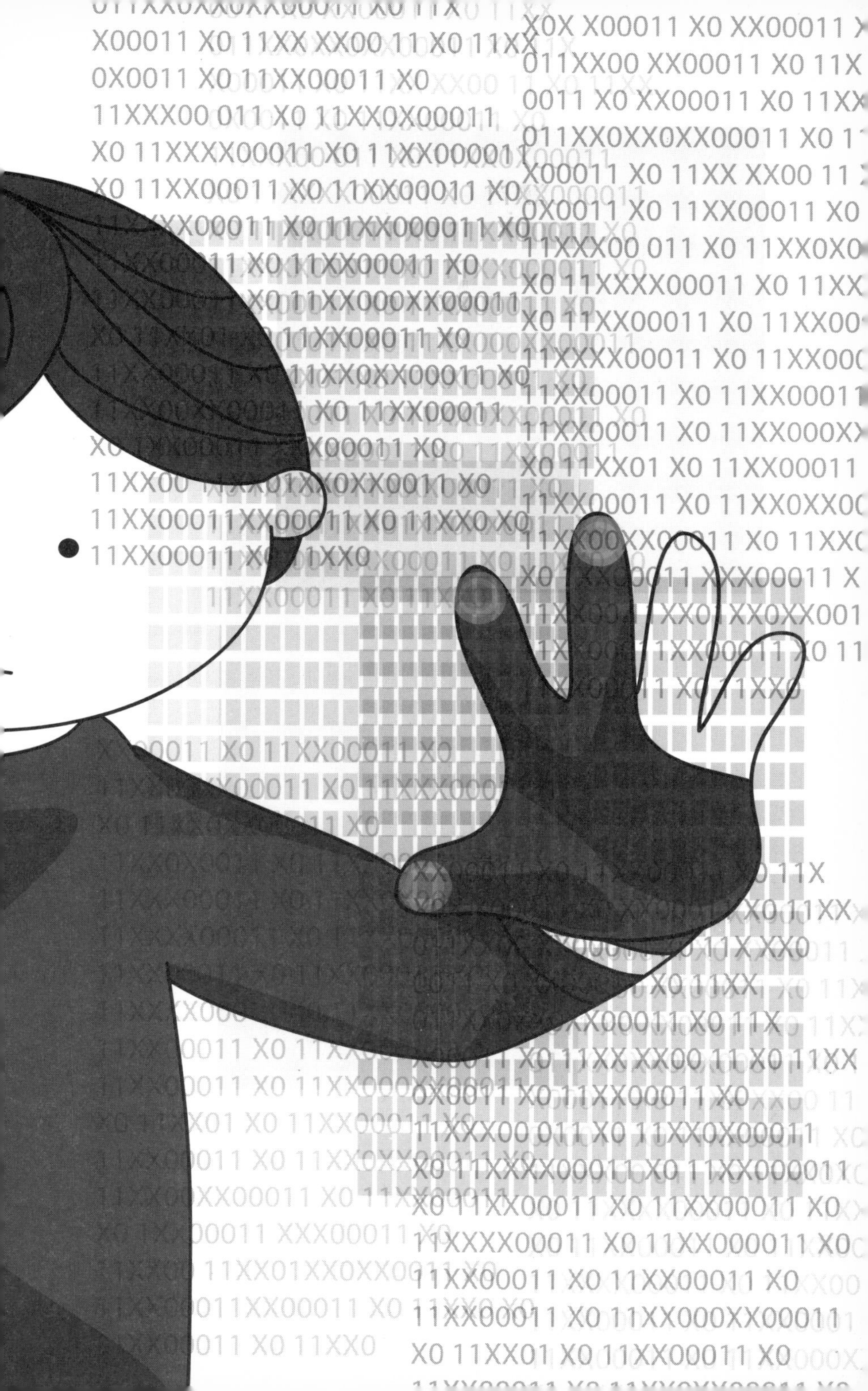

This is a summary of the personal information that you wouldn't mind your fans learning about you.

```
┌─────────────────┐
│                 │
│                 │
│   Your photo    │
│   goes here     │
│                 │
│                 │
└─────────────────┘
```

Full name in birth certificate:

_____

Nickname:

_____

Date of birth:_____ Star sign:_____

Country of birth:_____

Where you live:_____

_____

Height:_____

Names of siblings:

_____   _____

_____   _____

Names of best friends:

_____ _____ _____

_____ _____ _____

Pets:

Paste your pet's photo here	Paste your pet's photo here	Paste your pet's photo here

_____   _____

Languages you can speak:

_____   _____

Favourite sports:

_____   _____

_____   _____

Favourite songs:

_____   _____

_____   _____

Favourite movies:

_____   _____

_____   _____

Favourite colours:

_____ _____

Favourite TV show/cartoon:

_____ _____

_____ _____

Favourite stars you like:

_____ _____

_____ _____

Favourite food/drink:

_____ _____

_____ _____

Dislikes:

_____ _____

Phobia (Something that you're afraid of):

_____ _____

One secret trait no one knows about you:

_____

8
Take a Personality Test!

Congratulations! You've made it this far. Now let's do something different. Answer all the questions as truthfully as you can. After you're done, check your score against the table provided. This would give you a clue on how ready you are for fame.

1. Look at the three faces listed below. Circle the one which best reflects your mood most of the time.

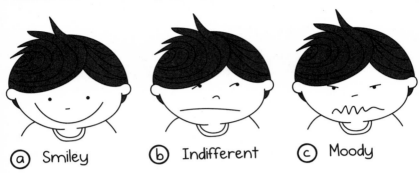

(a) Smiley   (b) Indifferent   (c) Moody

2. When you bomb in the toilet, how long do you take?

(a) 3 minutes (I don't like holding up the queue)

(b) 5 minutes (Oh man... It's agonising!)

(c) More than 15 minutes (Who says I'm constipated? I just need a private toilet!)

3. Here are five titles of classic children's books. Memorise the titles. Now close this diary, are you able to recall any or all of the titles?
   - *To Kill a Mockingbird* by Harper Lee
   - *Lord of the Flies* by William Golding
   - *The Chronicles of Narnia* by C. S. Lewis
   - *Where the Wild Things Are* by Maurice Sendak
   - *Guess How Much I Love You* by Sam McBratney

(a) Recalled all five titles

(b) Recalled two titles

(c) Can't remember any!

4. Say you're dressed in your worst tee and shorts, and you've put on a pair of shoes with a big hole in one. You forgot to brush your teeth in the morning, and you're feeling grumpy and hungry from having skipped breakfast. You step out of your flat and a flashbulb from a camera goes off in your face. What would you do?

(a) Smile and gamely say, "Give me five minutes, let me clean up and you can take a new picture of me!"

(b) You scream for your mother and tell her to call the police. You yell: "Paparazzi at the door!"

(c) You grab the nearest water hose and turn it on full blast at the photographer. You laugh with triumph when he runs away.

5. A member of the media asks you this difficult question. "Suppose you're trapped in a boat with your sister. There's a storm and the boat is sinking. There's only one life jacket in the boat. You have two choices to make, sacrifice yourself by jumping into the sea, thus lightening the load to save it from sinking further, or you throw your whiny, pesky and irritating sister off the boat and grab the life jacket for yourself." What's your answer?

(a) I need more time to think about the answer. I will get back to you after I've consulted my sister.

(b) Are you kidding? Throw her off the boat, of course.

(c) I won't be caught dead at sea with my sister. This is a stupid question.

6. This is one of the favourite questions judges like to ask of Beauty Queen Pageant Contestants: "If there's one wish that is granted to you by the Gods above, what would it be?"

(a) World peace for mankind. No more wars, suffering or abuse of children.

(b) Hmmm... can I have unlimited wishes? Am I clever or what?

(c) Can I wish for fame, money and a pimple-free complexion? That's one wish, as it's only one sentence.

7. You're on your way home after picking up a major award from a foreign land. Your plane has been delayed and you've been trapped in it for six hours. After an additional hour of waiting, your plane finally lands and you clear immigration and customs. You're so relieved to head home as you're exhausted. You leave the airport and find 200 fans waiting to root for you. What would you do?

(a) You smile and stop to shake a couple of hands and sign a few autographs. You apologise for not hanging around and you leave.

(b) You put on your sunglasses and wrap your head with your mother's scarf. You run for the waiting taxi and scoot, leaving your mother to deal with your fans.

(c) You walk right back into the airport and demand that the police escort you safely outside. You insist on taking the VIP exit route to avoid your fans.

8. On the day of a big performance, you receive two mystery gifts from your adoring fans. One is a lovely bouquet of 50 stalks of roses. The other gift is a box of luscious Belgian chocolates. Do you...

(a) motivate the people working with you by sharing the roses and chocolates with them.

(b) rip open the box of chocolates and gorge them all by yourself.

(c) scream for your personal assistant to throw away both the roses and chocolates, "I expect better from my fans!"

9. You're filming in the middle of the Sahara desert. The weather is 45 degrees celsius. The production assistant is taking lunch orders, you tell her you'd like to eat...

(a) whatever the director or crew are having.

(b) cold ice-cream served in a tall glass, with a cherry and an Oreo biscuit on the side.

(c) chocolate brownie served with two scoops of ice-cream, only vanilla flavour, please. Plus one huge glass of root beer with shaved ice, please.

Character Analysis Table

If your answers are mostly (a), then yes, you're ready for fame! You fit the shoes of a gracious, level-headed famous person. You may be young for fame, but you trust your mother to take care of you. More importantly, you understand that you need to stay humble in the face of challenges, and to smile and breeze through them.

If your answers are mostly (b), then you have to be wary. You're learning to handle fame when you're not mature enough for it. You need to watch and listen more, and seek the advice of an older person who's been through the game. Don't be afraid to ask someone for help if you can't deal with a situation arising from your fame.

If you've answered mostly (c), then I'm sorry to say that you're not cut out for fame. You get swept away easily, and you hurt others in your blunt approach to fame. Some people might even label you a "Diva". Maybe when you're older, you can get back on the pursuit of fame. For now, focus on your studies. Forget about being famous!

Disclaimer

From Amos Lee: I wrote the nine questions and designed the answers in this personality test. However, I DID NOT create the Character Analysis Table. My Mum did!

I'm sorry, I'm not even 13 yet, it's too difficult to read your character from the answers you've given. But I do hope you had fun answering them.

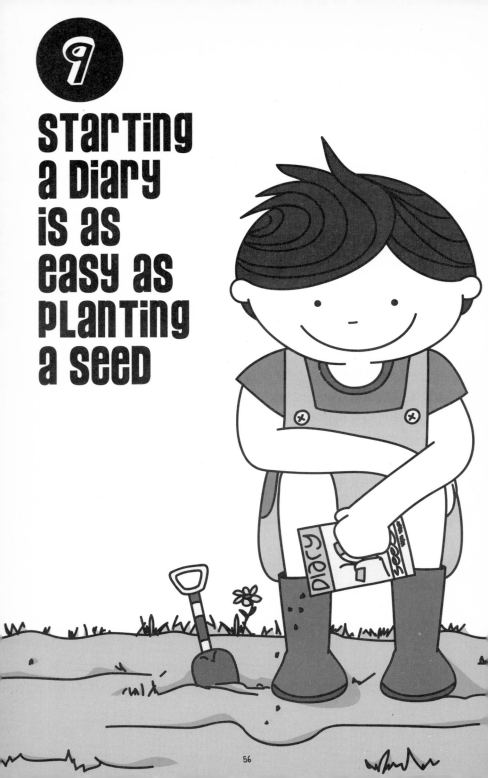

9

STarTing a Diary is as easy as planting a seed

Keep this diary filled with words and doodles. You never know when something might strike you. And when it does, writing it down helps to create more ideas. Have you ever planted seeds and watched them grow?

Writing a diary is like that! You write one page a day, and before you know it, you're hooked and writing more and more. Think of it as planting a seed. Add water and sunlight and watch it grow into a sapling, and then a big plant in no time!

Get Started Using These Ideas
One of the happiest moments of my life is...

_____

_____

_____

_____

_____

_____

Something that makes me laugh whenever I think about it.

_____

_____

_____

_____

_____

_____

My most embarrassing moment which I never
told anyone...

_____

_____

_____

_____

_____

_____

_____

When I'm sad, I feel like...

_____

_____

_____

_____

_____

_____

_____

10
FOR MOTHER
& DAUGHTER,
FATHER & SON

Use those ideas listed and ask your mother or father to fill your diary with their happiest moment, something that makes them laugh, their most embarrassing moment, or something that makes them sad. You'll be surprised when you read what they've written. Remember, they were once young, too. And like you, they've had their share of ups and downs.

For Mum or Dad
One of the happiest moments of my life is...

_____

_____

_____

_____

_____

_____

_____

Something that makes me laugh whenever I think about it.

_____

_____

_____

_____

_____

_____

_____

My most embarrassing moment which I never told anyone...

When I'm sad, I feel like...

amos Lee's gross & FUNNY STUFF FOR BOYS!

Rule No. 1 about being popular, you MUST be able to tell jokes. Have you ever wondered why people want to hang around a popular person?

Well, they're funny for one, and they make you feel good being their friend, right? Here're some gross and funny stuff you can share with your friends, but only with BOYS. Trust me, girls do not find these things funny. Don't ask me why!

TOILET SIGNS

Which of these do you like?

Chicks   Rooster

Snap and share your favourite toilet signs here!

If you're stuck in a forest and you need to go,
which of these positions would you pick?

Arm Power Squat

The Tree Support
Half Squat

Bum over Log Perch

Caveman Squat

POOP JOKES

Did You Know?

An elephant in a zoo was so seriously constipated that a zookeeper tried to feed it laxative foods. Nothing worked, so he resorted to pumping oil into its rectum! The method was so effective that the elephant discharged 90kg of faeces which landed on the keeper! Aaawww, man. How tragic!

POOP FACTS

Did You Know?

- The average weight of a poop is about 500 grammes.

- If you eat a lot of fatty foods, your poop will actually float! (But if you want to try this in the toilet, don't tell your mother Amos said you can eat lots of fried chicken wings! I don't want to be held responsible if your poop can't get flushed down the toilet.)

- If you eat a lot of meat, your poop will stink more!

- If you drink lots of milk and eat a lot of cheese and other dairy products, your poop will stink less than other people's. Hmmm... that explains why a baby's poop smells less stinky!

TEST YOUR BRAIN POWER!

Challenge Your Friends to Memorise
and Spell These Words

MUCUS

SNOT

PHLEGM

SPUTUM

NINCOMPOOP

Safe to Use Swear Words!
These words can be used in place of those that get your mother all riled up.

RATE YOUR TOLERANCE!

1. If asked to describe someone's "body odour", you say you don't worry about it, unless it smells like...

   (a) Stale cheese

   (b) Onions

   (c) Stinky socks

   (d) Pungent, salted fish

2. Which of these is the worst thing that can happen to you?

   (a) Sneezed on by an elephant.

   (b) Pooped on the head by a passing bird.

   (c) Stepping on monkey poop in the park.

   (d) Falling into a pile of elephant poop.

3. You're stuck in the toilet with no toilet paper. You forgot your handphone and can't call for help. It has been 30 minutes and there's no one around to save you. What would you do?

   (a) You continue waiting and hope for a miracle.

   (b) You remove a sock and wipe your bum with it.

c You remove your underwear, clean yourself and throw it away.

d You pull your trousers back on and run home to wash up.

4. In an enclosed space, like in a large lift, you are stuck with eight other people. Someone farts suddenly. It's so unbearably smelly that you look around to determine the culprit. You see the person looking red in the face, and you...

a catch him in the eye and give him a scowl.

b plug your nose and point an accusing finger at him.

c nudge the person closest to you and point a finger at the culprit, yelling, "It's him!"

d utter, "Someone ate durians for supper last night!"

Now check your answers. If they're mostly d, well, congratulations, you're someone with a high tolerance level. Chances are, you would be someone who has many friends! You can accept your friends' shortcomings and when faced with a problem or obstacle, you embrace it, smile and get on with overcoming it.

RATE YOUR POOP!

Which is the King of Poop?

Lumpies or "Deer Poop"

Lame

Baby Ruth
Poop that looks
chock-full of nuts.

Cute

The Brown Sausage
Perfect poop that slips
out in a nice long shape.

Feat ⭐⭐⭐

Yoghurt Express
The splash poop.
What a big mess!

Gross ★

The Runny Brown Jam
This is the type that you
don't want to pass out
in school!

Eeiuuw... ★

The Snake Coil
Need I say more?

Super Feat
★ ★ ★ ★

Machine Pellets
Stools that shoot out
like a machine gun!

Awesome!
★ ★ ★ ★ ★

76

12

THE AMOS LEE GUIDE TO RELIEVING CONSTIPATION!

The dictionary defines constipation as "the condition of being unable to empty the bowels frequently enough or effectively".

I'm sure this is one inconvenience everyone understands! Have you ever felt like you can't get anything done because you're "stuck" or sitting on, well, "something" inside you?

Fret not! I have created three recipes guaranteed to help you relieve your inconvenience. If none of this works, what you need to do is to visit the pharmacy to buy something labelled as "laxative".

But seriously, if you are still unable to find something that helps get the poop out, please see the doctor.

THE BREAKFAST SMOOTHIE

Makes 3 cups (for very constipated victims)

Ingredients:

100g papaya, cut into cubes

I large banana, cut into pieces

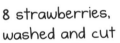

8 strawberries, washed and cut

125g crushed ice

100g blueberries, washed

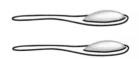

180ml fresh milk

125ml freshly squeezed orange juice

2 tbsp of honey

Instructions:

1. Place all the ingredients in a blender and blend until smooth. Remember to keep the lid on before you press the start button!

2. Serve and drink.

3. If by the end of the day you still don't see the potency of this concoction, try it again. This time, double the amount of bananas and milk. Seriously, if you still can't poop by nightfall, you need to see the doctor.

THE SOFT PRETZEL

What's this? It's a biscuit baked
in the shape of a stick or a loose knot.
It's popular in Southern Germany as well as in some areas
of America. For taste, it can be seasoned with sugar glaze
or salt. Seeds or nuts can also be added for texture.

Er... you may ask why is the pretzel featured here?
Well, look long and hard at the shape of the pretzel I've
drawn, does it remind you of something that gets passed
out in the toilet? Aaha!

Ingredients:

250ml
warm milk
(microwave
for one
minute)

3 tbsp butter, melted

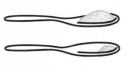

1 1/4 tsp
instant
dry yeast

1 tsp salt

1 1/2 tbsp dark
brown sugar

1 tbsp honey

450g plain flour

1 small egg
(beaten for glazing)

Instructions:

1. Preheat the oven to 180 degrees Celsius.

2. Sift the flour and salt.

3. In a large mixing bowl, combine the warm milk, honey and dry yeast and let the mixture stand for about 10 minutes.

4. Add the sugar to the flour mixture, knead into a ball until smooth.

5. Grease a bowl with some oil. Place the dough in it and slightly dab the top of the dough with a little oil. Cover the bowl with a plastic wrap. Leave it in a warm place, let the dough ferment overnight!

6. When the dough has risen to twice its size, knead it a few more times to let air out (if you're wondering why the dough has expanded, it's not magic, it's just the yeast doing its job).

7. Roll the dough into a long strip. Form a "U" shape with it and then twist both ends inwards so that they overlap in the middle. Press both ends to the bottom. Now you have a pretzel!

8. Place the pretzels on an ungreased cookie pan. Brush the top with some of the beaten egg.

9. Bake for about 25 - 30 minutes till brown. Remove from the oven and spread with melted butter. Sprinkle some salt before serving!

Try eating the pretzel when it's warm. Don't think too much about the original version inspired by a large toilet moment!

If you still haven't figured out what this reminds you of, you are obviously a "One-Star Poop Rating" non-achiever. (Refer to page 74 for complete ratings)

The Famous Amos Contender

So I'm named after the cookies. What can be cornier than to have people ask, "Can you bake famous cookies?" Are they kidding me? My cookies are the best in town! At least WPI and Everest think so.

THE ALL-CHOCOLATE AMOS LEE COOKIES

Ingredients:

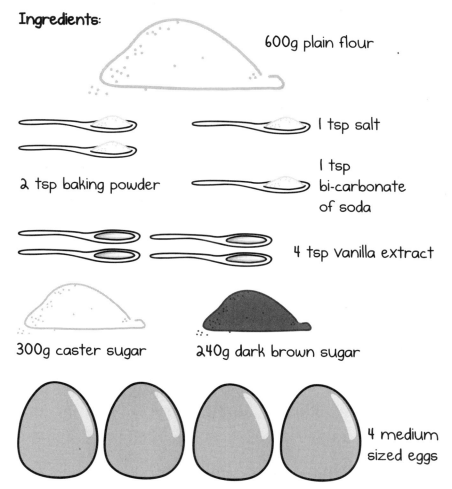

600g plain flour

1 tsp salt

2 tsp baking powder

1 tsp bi-carbonate of soda

4 tsp vanilla extract

300g caster sugar

240g dark brown sugar

4 medium sized eggs

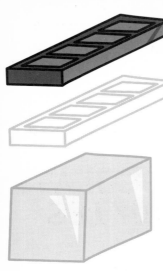 200g dark chocolate, melted

300g white chocolate, melted

 600g cocoa flavoured chips

500g unsalted butter

Instructions:

1. Preheat oven to 160 degrees Celsius for 10 minutes. Line cookie trays with baking paper.

2. Sift the flour, baking powder, bi-carbonate of soda and salt.

3. Use an electric mixer and cream the butter and sugar for about 5 minutes.

4. Add eggs (slightly beaten), one at a time and beat for 20 seconds after each addition.

5. Add the vanilla extract and melted dark chocolate. Blend well!

6. On low speed, add the flour mixture in 3 batches. Scrape down the sides of the mixing bowl, and then at low speed, add the cocoa chips and melted white chocolate, mix well.

7. Drop about 2 tablespoons of batter onto the cookie trays. Place them 2 inches apart (to leave room to expand, duh!). Bake for about 25 - 30 minutes until the cookies are golden brown.

8. Leave cookies on the tray for about 2 minutes before cooling them on a rack.

And that's it! End of this section. Save those cookies as a treat after you've bombed. Happy blending and baking! Remember, I'm the real Famous Amos.

13
Tips From Whoopie Lee

ARE YOU A STAR?

Everyone is a star. It's just inside you, waiting to reveal itself. What's really important is to "Believe in Yourself!" Remember the following:

1. **Your talent makes you unique!**
   You're special, don't ever doubt that!

2. **Practise! Practise! Practise!**
   Whatever you do, it's diligent practice that makes you better. Whether it's doing exam papers or learning a new song and dance, practice makes perfect.

3. **Have fun!**
   It's important to have fun because if you don't, then why are you doing it? If you enjoy yourself, your fans or followers will, too!

4. Here're four lines you can remember to make yourself feel strong. Say these lines every day before you go to bed.

I AM SPECIAL
I AM COOL
I AM A STAR
I TOTALLY RULE!

What Songs Perk You Up?

Album/Song Title: Artist:

_____   _____

_____   _____

_____   _____

_____   _____

_____   _____

_____   _____

_____   _____

_____   _____

_____   _____

_____   _____

_____   _____

_____   _____

_____   _____

When you're feeling down, choose songs that help to perk you up! Here're some I like!

- *Firework* by Katy Perry

- *Through The Rain* by Mariah Carey

- *A Moment Like This* by Kelly Clarkson

- *The Climb* by Miley Cyrus

- *Change* by Taylor Swift

- *You Are Not Alone* by Michael Jackson

- *Don't Worry Be Happy* by Bobby McFerrin

- *Baby* by Justin Bieber

STRIKE A POSE!

Do you stand tall or do you slouch? If you imagine yourself as a mountain, which exudes confidence and strength, you'll feel taller.

Here's an easy pose. Stand with your back against the wall. Try to align the back of your heels against the wall. Can you feel the stretch on your back muscles?

THE MOUNTAIN POSE

- Relax your mind.

- Keep your eyes focused on something pleasant.

- Roll your shoulders back and relax your arms.

- Your feet should be flat on the ground and a ruler's length (about 30cm) apart.

- Inhale deeply and exhale.

- Do this for ten minutes.

Do you feel more relaxed? Try this pose whenever you're feeling anxious or excited. It helps to calm your nerves, especially before a big event!

THE SITTING YOGI

- Sit with your legs crossed.

- Close your eyes.

- Rest both hands on your belly, one hand above the belly button and one below.

- Breathe in and fill your belly with air, just like a balloon. Breathe out and feel your belly deflate.

- Try to count each breath quietly.

- If your mind wanders, start counting from one again. Repeat this till you feel relaxed.

THE TREE POSE

- Stand like in the mountain pose. Focus your eyes on a spot a few feet in front of you.

- Shift your body weight to your right leg; now raise your left foot off the ground.

- Open your left knee out to the side and place your left foot on your inner thigh just above your right knee. Breathe, focus and stand tall.

- Raise your arms out to the side so that your arms are in a straight line, parallel to the ground. Imagine they are like branches of a tree.

- Hold this balance. If you're comfortable, try raising your arms higher till your palms touch above your head.

That's it! You've just mastered three simple yoga poses to help you relax. For someone who seeks fame, it's important to keep yourself cool and grounded. Try any of these poses any time you feel anxious. And let me share with you a secret. The tree pose is something that most boys find difficult to do.

Try it against your big brother. Bet he'll topple over! So there are things that girls can do better than boys. Isn't that great?

 # WHOOPIE LEE'S PAGE FOR GIRLS

TAKE THE TALENT TEST!

Do You Have What It Takes to Be a Star?

1. You're taking piano lessons and your teacher tells you to practise for 30 minutes every day. Do you...

   (a) listen and obey her, but you practise for more than 30 minutes every day.

   (b) practise ten minutes every day.

   (c) practise for five minutes each day, if you remember.

2. You've been given a role in a concert performance. Two hours before the show, you sprain your ankle. What do you do?

   (a) Pop a sweet in your mouth, ask your mother to bandage your ankle and decide to give it your best shot!

   (b) Complain about your bad luck, when you get to school, you remind your cast members that they can't go on without you.

   (c) You call the teacher in charge and insist that the show is cancelled. It cannot go on without you because you have a sprained ankle.

3. You're on stage performing a song for Children's Day. Suddenly, you forget your lyrics! You...

(a) make up words and hum along, still smiling cheerily.

(b) laugh and stop the song.

(c) drop your mike and scream at the pianist, you ask to be excused, saying it's the pianist's fault, "She hit the wrong key!"

4. You and your best friend are performing a dance routine. A few days before the performance, you notice that she's A LOT BETTER than you. You decide to...

(a) tell her how great she is doing and ask her to help you.

(b) sulk and secretly wish that she stumbles and falls.

(c) tell her that she looks fat and dancing makes her look lame.

If you answered mostly (a), then wow, you're ready to be a star! You're a gracious person and you have a great attitude towards learning. Work hard on your talent, remember, practice makes perfect, you will get far one day!

ESTABLISH A TRADEMARK LOOK!

Create a Style that's Uniquely You....

GIRL-NEXT-DOOR

SMARTY-PANTS

ROCK STAR

Which of these "looks" do you like? Look for clothes that make you feel fabulous! But don't try to be someone you're not. More importantly, you must have fun and believe in yourself!

Create your own unique look. Think about your hairstyle, a favourite outfit and accessories to put on.

CULTIVATE A TALENT!

Are you good at playing the piano, violin or maybe the guitar? Or maybe you love to sing and dance. Someone who's not musically inclined may be better at sports, like playing badminton or netball.

Whatever it is, cultivate a talent that will make you stand out. It isn't good enough to have perfect scores in your examinations. Remember, you'll need to be an all-rounder* to be a star!

*From the dictionary: **All-rounder**
Someone who has the ability in many things, especially in sports.

What skill do you want to learn?

_____

_____

Why do you want to learn this new skill?

_____

_____

What skill do you want to learn?

_____

_____

Why do you want to learn this new skill?

_____

_____

What skill do you want to learn?

_____

_____

Why do you want to learn this new skill?

_____

_____

GET LISTED IN A
BOOK OF RECORDS!

Have you ever admired people who are able to do things that make others go "WOW"?

Here's a secret. Everyone loves a show-off. Especially if the person can do something that no one else can. And I'm not talking about flying, duh.

It could be something like having the ability to walk backwards without tripping, or shoot a basketball hoop and get the ball in with your eyes closed!

Here's a list of abilities that most kids can't do. If you can adopt these and execute them, I guarantee you that you'll be famous in no time!

Roll your tongue (It has to fold sideways. Look in the mirror as you do it. Do not, and I repeat, DO NOT, use your fingers!)

Sneeze with your eyes open.

Put one hand on the head and pat it. Now rub your tummy with the other hand at the same time. Can you do it?

Lick your own elbow. Your tongue must touch the tip of the elbow!

Raise one eyebrow. No cheating, not both eyebrows, just ONE! Now twitch your nose or wriggle your ears. (If you can do this, you deserve to enter your name in a Book of Records!)

Touch your nose or chin with your tongue. (Seriously, I don't know anyone who is able to do this! Try not to dribble too much saliva all over yourself.)

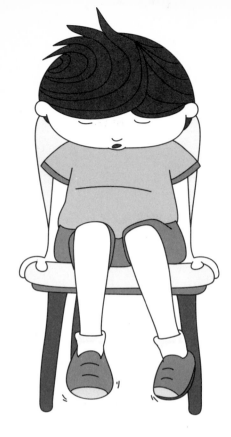

Sit down and circle one foot in a clockwise direction while using the other foot to write the number '9'. Move both feet at the same time! No pause allowed!

Are you able to do any of these feats?
If you are, congratulations! You're going to be famous!
However, if you find yourself unable to speak because you've twisted your tongue or strained a facial muscle, don't blame me.

Have fun practising these superhuman abilities!

16 THE AMOS LEE "HOW TO BE A SUPERHERO" GUIDE

Have you ever nurtured a desire to star in a TV show or a movie as a superhero? This is your chance to be one. Look no further than this diary!

You must be bigger than any of the superheroes ever created. You must be original. You must be totally imaginative! You must be the one and only, Super Pretzel Hero! Duh, you say? Oh pleeeasssuzeee.

Wait till you reach the end of this section. I promise you this is really fun. Imagine yourself as the world's greatest heroic creation. Better than a certain Mr. Lee who created the superhero that got bitten by a spider. Lame.

Pick an alphabet _____

You are SUPER PRETZEL "_____" HERO
Now draw it like a pretzel and this will
be your new identity!

Draw how you would like to look

What is your GOAL as a Super Pretzel Hero?

_____

_____

_____

_____

_____

_____

_____

If you have a secret weapon or accessory to help you
in your goal, what will it be?

_____

_____

_____

_____

_____

Draw/Design your secret
weapon or accessory

What is your weakness? (For Superman, it's kryptonite. For me, it's when Whoopie yells, "Muuuuummmmm, see what Amos did!")

_____

_____

_____

_____

_____

Is there something embarrassing about you that no one knows? (I know someone who still sucks on her thumb to lull herself to sleep. Hmmm... not telling who. But here's a hint, she shares the same last name as me)

_____

_____

_____

_____

_____

_____

_____

Here's the last part. Pretend that you're this Super Pretzel Hero for a day. Assume his or her personality totally.

My name is...

_____

_____

I am the World's Greatest...

_____

_____

My goal in life is to...

_____

_____

_____

_____

_____

_____

Pick Your Favourite Ones

Here's what I like to do in school:

○ Fight bullies (only by scolding them behind their backs)

○ Defend girls (or wimps) from bullies smaller in size than me

○ Look good in tights (underwear must be worn on the outside, it's a tradition, duh!)

○ Ask intelligent questions to irritate teachers

○ Keep asking to go to the toilet every 15 minutes to check that no bullies are lurking around

I have superhuman abilities. I can:

○ Roll my tongue

○ Sneeze with my eyes open

○ Lick my own elbow

○ Put one hand on the head and pat it while rubbing my tummy with the other hand at the same time

○ Sit down and circle one foot in a clockwise direction while using the other foot to write the number '9'

○ I can touch my nose or chin with my tongue

○ I can raise one eyebrow, twitch my nose or wriggle my ears

○ I can stretch both arms like a pretzel to have my fingers meet at the back

Now write a diary entry with the opening line

"And henceforth I shall dominate the school as the world's Greatest Super Pretzel Hero. I promise to..."

_____

_____

_____

_____

_____

_____

_____

_____

_____

Well, congratulations for making it this far! Now you're officially the World's Most Incredible Super Pretzel Hero.

Have fun with this character. One day, you'll outgrow it and find yourself a new role to assume in a TV show or a movie. But till that happens, stay famous as the cartoon drawn in this diary!

17 VOLUNTEER

Do You Volunteer?

Do you feel that you have a lot in life to be thankful for? Well, some people don't. So if you have time and you want to help those less fortunate than you, you're on the right track to becoming a star.

Most famous people make time to volunteer with a charity. Their celebrity status helps to bring attention to a situation that needs urgent attention, like raise funds for victims of an earthquake, or collect donations to build a school in a poor country.

As a student, you can start by taking small steps. Support your teachers in community clean-up or recycling projects. Visit old folks' homes or orphanages to cheer up the residents. Do something small, it goes a long way.

Check Out These Websites if You Wish to Volunteer

The National Volunteer Centre Singapore
www.nvpc.org.sg
www.sgcares.org

Volunteer Singapore
www.volunteersingapore.com

This is it. This is the last page of the *D.I.Y. Toilet Diary to Fame!* This is only the beginning of your first step to fame. Keep on writing and remember, you learnt it from us here. All the best!

amos Lee

About the Author

Adeline Foo has a Master of Fine Arts from New York University's Tisch School of the Arts (Asia). She lives in Singapore with her husband and three children.

Adeline counts creating new recipes as her second love after writing. Her current obsession is creating whoopie pies! Inspired by Whoopie Lee, also known as Whiny, Pesky and Irritating, or WPI, by Amos, she is starting an online bake shop with a friend, Allan Teoh, who has provided the recipes for Amos' cookies and pretzels in this book.

If you are curious to know more about the whoopie pie, write to her at www.amoslee.com.sg, or visit www.allanbakes.com.